In honor of Tom, my husband, Frances, my mother, and all those who have given of their time and substance to Bridges of Faith to share the love of God with Ukrainian orphans.

In memory of David, an orphan who visited Bridges of Faith Camp in Alabama and who became a follower of God. Not adopted, David enlisted in the Ukrainian army. He sadly lost his life defending his country from the Russian invasion.

A portion of the proceeds from each book will go toward Bridges of Faith's orphanage and K-12 school in Romania for Ukrainian orphan refugees. When Russia invaded Ukraine, many orphans fled the country for safety. Bridges of Faith serves these children.

Copyright © 2024 by Nancy Elizabeth Benz

All rights reserved. No part of this publication may be reproduced, distributed, or transmittled by any means, including photocopying, recording, or any other electronic or mechanical methods, without the prior written permission of the author, except in the case of brief quotations embodied in critical reviews and certain other noncommercial uses permitted by copyright law.

For permission requests, write to nancy@bridgesoffaith.com or benz@bridgesoffaith.com

Five Stones Publishing**, Fairhope, NY 14450** - randyjohnson@ilncenter.com or randy2905@gmail.com

ISBN 978-1-945423-65-9

First Edition

Printed in the United States of America

Publsher's Cataloging in Publication Data

Names: Benz, Nancy Long, author

Title: Jane, Found on Jane Lane/Nancy Long Benz

Description: First Edition | Fairport< NY: Five Stones Publishing

benz@bridgesoffaith.com | bridgesoffaith.com

www.servicedogjane.com

JANE
Found on Jane Lane

By Nancy Long Benz

Illustrated by Kidsbook Art LLC

Part One

Jane Finds her Forever Home

My name is Jane. I'm a Rhodesian Ridgeback dog. All of us Ridgebacks have hair down the middle of our backs that stands straight up and makes a ridge. We are often trained to hunt lions in Africa.

This athletic breed loves to run and makes excellent family guardians. - American Kennel Club

As a puppy, I didn't chase lions or have other great adventures. I was an orphan. You know, I didn't have a mom or dad. I remember being scared, hungry and lonely . . . wishing I had a human like the other dogs. I watched as their human masters played with them, throwing frisbees in the park.

Orphans are children who usually live in a children's home with caregivers.

As for me, I ate food I found in garbage cans and I got yelled at just for being a stray dog.

One morning I aimlessly wondered around, feeling especially lonely. I noticed a human man jogging on Jane Lane. He gave me a quick smile! My tail almost wagged off in excitement. I ran with him until he picked me up and stroked my back. He took me home, fed me and cared for me. His name was Major Benz!

Major Benz was my first human friend. His kindness has always been stored in my dog memory. He is my human hero forever. After all, he rescued me!

One night, Major Benz quietly told me he was going to be deployed. That's a human military word for being sent away on a mission . . . without his family. Major Benz sadly said he couldn't bring me along .

He said, "My dad will care for you and protect you. You will grow to love Mr. Tom, just as I do!"

As long as a dog can smell, see and hear, dogs most likely will remember you, no matter how long you have been out of their lives. - www.hola.com

I went to live with Mr. Tom at Bridges of Faith. The land was like nothing I had ever seen! It was lush and spacious! Surrounded by nature, the sweet smelling pine trees gave me hiding places while I chased woodland animals.

My donkey friend loved playing with me. I splashed in her drinking water and you could hear the echo of 'hee-haw" all through the camp as I chased her . . . until she started chasing me! This was paradise for a dog like me.

Every day I played with the children who lived at the camp. They rode with their dad in a golf cart while he worked. I loved racing alongside them! I always outran the golf cart while the children cheered me on.

As wonderful as it all was, there were difficult times. My curious spirit sometimes made me break rules.

Being a post orphan stray dog, I had trouble obeying the new rules. Mr. Tom had to train me to be an obedient dog. I tried hard to obey because I wanted to please him. I had an unswerving (human word for constant) loyalty and dedication to him.

One of my first golden rules on the property . . . "NO POTTY BREAKS INSIDE BUILDINGS!" I would go to time out as soon as I would potty in the wrong spot! I caught on quickly!

One brisk night, I carefully sneaked out of the house, breaking the rule—"DO NOT GO OUT AFTER DARK!" I couldn't help myself! I loved the cool night air. As I chased a squirrel up a tree, several coyotes spotted me. When I heard the coyotes give their frightful "owwoooo," I knew I was in trouble.

I leaped through the woods as fast as my long legs would carry me. I finally made it back to the camp. Mr. Tom was not happy with me at all!! I understood very well what Mr. Tom was teaching me. "RULES ARE FOR YOUR PROTECTION! What a teachable moment!

Mrs. Christal, our cook at the camp, held a special place in my heart. I could smell her yummy food miles away. She taught me a rule that I quickly learned. "DO NOT EVER GO IN THE KITCHEN!"

For me, there was an imaginary line between the dining hall and the kitchen. I would lay with my paws up against that line, but not over it. Mrs. Christal gave me snacks of human food for being obedient.

A dog has been known to smell people and other odors up to 12 miles away, depending on wind and the type of scent.

www.ark-valley.org

I had many human friends at the camp. I would stroll into Mr. Tom's special meetings and be greeted by so many friends . . . even the ones I could tell did not really like dogs!

It was fun watching them pretend to like me. After all, my human master was Mr. Tom, the President of Bridges of Faith. No one was allowed to mess with me! Mr. Tom just wouldn't allow it.

Every morning I would lick Mr. Tom's feet to awaken him. He would gently pet me saying. "Jane, you're the best dog in the world! You're the fastest dog in the world! You're the smartest dog in the world!" And I believed every word!

When Mr. Tom was away, I would watch out the office window anxiously waiting for his return. My keen ears could hear his truck miles away coming back to the camp. I was so excited when he drove through the gate. I wanted to leap through the window!

Dogs can hear four times more than humans. They can hear a wider range of frequencies. They can hear your heartbeat from across the room. www.wagwalking.com

Part Two

Jane Becomes a Therapy Dog

Early one rainy morning, I sprawled out on the front porch, enjoying the smell of the rain.

I carefully listened as Mr. Tom softly spoke. He said, "Jane, I'm going to give you an important job. You will wear a beautiful special service dog vest. You will be a therapy dog for orphans."

After training, I finally wore my special vest and met the children at the airport. I was so excited to greet them. I stood very still so they would know it was OK to pet me. Tiny fingers stroked my ridge down to my tail. I made the children feel safe and comfortable.

I DID MY JOB!!

One day, I saw an angry looking girl. Mr. Tom introduced me to her. As she petted me, her face softened into a smile. Mr. Tom asked her to look after me. She thought she helped me, but I helped her become a pleasant girl.

MY WORK WAS DONE!

I sensed that these children were frightened, lonely and scared—just like I felt before I was rescued. They really wanted human heroes, just like I did. After all, I am Jane, once an orphan, found on Jane Lane.

The children would come to camp and to see how we live. I proudly escorted them to many places, like beautiful parks.

This is PEACH PARK in Clanton, Alabama . . .

... TO THE SPACE AND ROCKET CENTER ...

One special day, Anna, a child who visited us before, came to the camp. I loved it when she attacked me with hugs. I gave her my best doggy kisses! She found her wonderful forever home with Jack and Elizabeth. My eyes, like hers, gleamed with excitement.

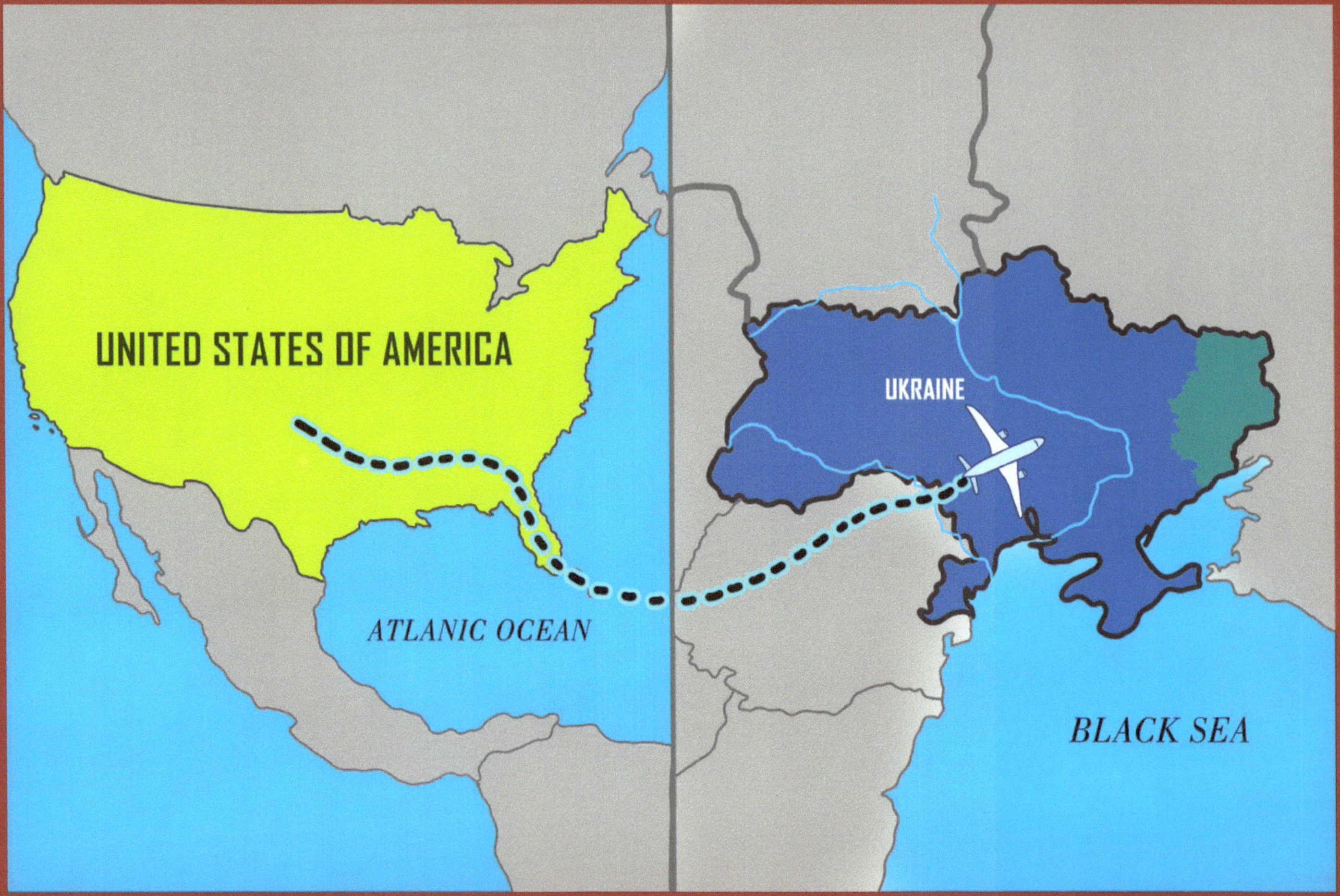

Jack flew to Ukraine to adopt Anna. He heroically rescued her as Russia prepared to invade. He became her hero as Major Benz and Mr. Tom were my heroes.

There is an imaginary bridge of faith between the US and Ukraine. That's why we call ourselves Bridges of Faith.

As Anna stroked me, I wanted to tell her that everything may not be easy at first, especially with the new rules. I wanted to tell her that the rules are to keep her safe. She needed to know that when her human parents scold her, that means they love her. But I knew that she would learn — just as I did.

I understood her . . . after all, I'm Jane the orphan dog, found on Jane Lane.

I did my important job, I fulfilled my purpose to be kind to those in need.

Just like me, you have a unique purpose. Whatever that is, always remember, "Be kind to one another!"

The End

The adventures of Jane at Bridges of Faith, the adoptive Service Dog, are actual happenings. Jane has worked with orphans as a Service Animal since 2016. Since the Russian invaded Ukraine, Bridges of Faith has not been able to bring children to Alabama, therefore Jane has transformed into a service animal in other areas.

About the Author . . .

A native of Alabama, Nancy Benz spent 25 years in elementary school classrooms. After retiring, she began working with Ukrainian orphans at Bridges of Faith in Clanton, Alabama, where she currently serves as Director of Ministries.

Nancy says she felt two distinct callings from God, one to teach and another to minister to orphans. (James 1:27) "Religion that God our Father accepts as pure and faultless is this: to look after orphans and widows in their distress and to keep oneself from being polluted by the world."

Nancy holds a master's degree in elementary education and is National Board Certified. Nancy and her husband, Tom, President and Founder of Bridges of Faith, live together with Jane in Chilton County, Alabama, with plenty of room for Jane to roam.

www.ingramcontent.com/pod-product-compliance
Lightning Source LLC
Chambersburg PA
CBHW060759090426
42736CB00002B/91